CW01656374

Affiliate Marketing for Beginners

7 Steps to Earning $200+ in less than 25 Hours a Week

Table of Contents

Introduction

Chapter 1 – First Step - Understanding Affiliate Marketing

Chapter 2 – Second Step – Getting Started

Chapter 3 – Third Step – Understanding Search Engine Optimisation

Chapter 4 – Fourth Step – Optimising Your Website/Blog for Search Engines

Chapter 5 – Fifth Step – Choosing an Affiliate Program

Chapter 6 – Sixth Step – Selecting Products

Chapter 7 – Seventh Step – Building a Database of Users/Customers

Conclusion

BONUS BOOK: Start an Ebay Business

Introduction

I want to thank you and congratulate you for downloading the book, Affiliate Marketing for Beginners.

This book contains proven steps and strategies on how to make more than $2000 a month in less than 25 hours a week.

Affiliate marketing is one of the easiest ways to make money online. Once you are set up and properly promoting the products, it becomes an excellent way of generating substantial passive income. Most people jump into affiliate marketing without knowing the basics and therefore do not have much success. In this book, you will learn about what affiliate marketing is, which products to promote, where to promote them, how to setup, search engine optimise, and promote your blog and website to earn money through affiliate marketing programs.

Thanks again for downloading this book, I hope you enjoy it!

Chapter 1 – First Step - Understanding Affiliate Marketing

There are many ways in which people can make money on the Internet, like pay per click and other advertisements, but it is difficult to make a decent income in these ways. They require a great a deal of work but the earnings are very little, and that is why people are turning to affiliate marketing; it allows people to easily make a lot of money, over $2000 per month. In affiliate marketing, a way of advertising on the Internet, people become affiliated with other online businesses or website owners through different affiliate programs, and help generate leads, traffic, and sales for those businesses. When they help the business make a sale, they get commission for it. In simple words, you help people sell their products, and in return, they pay you a fixed percentage from the total cost of each product sold. The more products you help them sell, the more you earn. The affiliate marketing practice is very popular among small companies, online businesses, as well as new business.

Difference Between Pay Per Click and Affiliate Marketing

With Pay Per Clicks, you place the ads for a product, business, or website on your own blog or website and promote them; this helps those businesses generate organic traffic. Every time someone clicks on one of the ads on your website, you earn money for it; the amount you earn is usually in cents. (A typical example of pay per click is Google AdSense.) In contrast to that, in affiliate marketing you can promote the products all you want but you do not earn anything for the clicks. Whatever money you make only comes from the products that people purchase from them through your channel. So, if you are advertising a $500 product and the business has agreed to pay you a 20% from the sale, then for each product you help them sell, you will make $100. The sales may not be as many as the clicks, but even a few sales can generate way more money for you than hundreds of clicks.

The affiliate programs usually offer payments in three ways, which are:

Cost Per Click or CPC

In this model of payment, a user visiting your website will see the advertisement and click on it to go to the merchant's website. You will earn money for this click, and the payment is usually in cents.

Cost Per Lead or CPL

In this model of payment, a user visiting your website will see the advertisement and go to the merchant's website by clicking on it, and then will fill out a form on the merchant's website. You will earn money for every form that is filled.

Cost Per Sale or CPS

In this model of payment, a user visiting your website will see the advertisement and go to the merchant's website through it and buy their product. You will earn a fixed percentage from the sale of every product that gets sold this way. The percentage of the profit you will get is usually between 4% to 20%.

Chapter 2 – Second Step – Getting Started

To get started and join an affiliate program, the first thing you will need is a solid platform. In this guide, we will focus on a websites and blogs. It has been seen that some people affiliate themselves with one business or product and focus solely on promoting it. If it is a product that sells well or you are getting 20% or reasonable profits from it then it might be a good idea, but having a general website or blog is also preferred as it does not limit your scope and leaves room for promoting different products. The more products and businesses you get affiliated with, the higher your chances of making profits are. One product can limit the scope but having more than one affiliates can't, so we recommend that.

The first thing you will need to do is create a blog or a website.

Creating A Blog:

The first thing you need to make your own blog is a host. You can go for free blogs as well, but those are limiting in scope and most of them already come with advertisements and only give you a limited control. Having your only blog means that you get full control over it, and you will not get any advertisement from the host. You can find a good blog hosting for less than $5 a month, and given the profits that you can make, this cost becomes negligible.

The next thing you need to do is get a domain for your blog. Unlike web hosting, a domain is bought for at least a year although the prices for domains are very low. You can get a domain from GoDaddy.com for less than $10 per year. Your domain is the link that people will use to go to your website, and it can be anything, like www.yourwebsite.com. It is also important to choose your domain wisely because domain serves SEO purposes and also gives people an idea of what your website/blog is about. If you plan on affiliating with health products, you can go for something like www.healthylife.com, www.healthproducts.com, etc. Just make sure that your domain is able to convey what your blog is about.

After getting a domain and a hosting, since you are setting up a blog, you need to install WordPress. There are several other blogging softwares available on the Internet but WordPress is one of the most popular and widely used ones, and it is also very easy to use. If your hosting offers WordPress installation, go for it, as they will already have everything set up. Otherwise, you can go to www.wordpress.org and download the software from there and install it.

After installing WordPress, once you are ready, you will have to select a theme. WordPress offers several different themes for free. You can preview each theme and then select the design that best suits your blogging needs. Select a theme that puts the blog content in the centre but also leaves some room for the affiliates.

Once everything is set up and ready to go, login to your WordPress to start blogging. The link for that is usually www.(yourdomain).com/wp-admin/. From there on, you can start writing posts for your blog.

Creating A Website:

To create a website, the first two steps are the same as above. You need to find a hosting and get a domain name. Most good website hosts offer free templates and website making wizards to guide you in making your website. You can also find free templates for your website on the Internet.

Even if you opt for a website, it is important to have a blog for SEO purposes. We will cover them in the next chapter.

Chapter 3 – Third Step – Understanding Search Engine Optimisation

The dictionary definition of Search Engine Optimisation is:

Search Engine Optimisation (SEO) is the process of affecting the visibility of a website in a search engine's 'natural' or 'organic' search results."

In Affiliate Marketing, you make money by helping other businesses sell their products. To help them sell products, you need to tell people about their products, and you do that through your website or blog. But you need to bring people to your own website or blog first. New websites or blogs are usually difficult for people to find. How would anyone know that you have created one? If people want something, they search for it on search engines like Yahoo, Bing, Google, etc. And you not only need to get your website on a search engine, you need to make it rank higher so that it shows up on the first page of results and people find it easily.

Why Search Engine Optimisation is Important

When you search for something on a search engine, like Google, the results you see are search engine optimised. Optimising your website for a search engine improves its visibility and makes it easy for the search engines to find it, and for the people to find your website, page, or business. The most well-optimised websites are on the front page. Most people never look beyond the first three pages on a search engine. When you search for something, you get tens of pages with results. If your website is somewhere in the middle or the end, the chances of anyone finding your website are pretty slim. That is precisely why you need to optimise your website for search engines, and bring it to the front page.

Chapter 4 – Fourth Step – Optimising Your Website/Blog for Search Engines

Following are the main things that you need to keep in mind when optimising your page for search engines.

Keywords are words that people use when searching for something on the internet. During 'Search and Match,' the keywords a person searches with are matched with the content on your website/blog, so it is very important to make sure that you have the right keywords on your page.

You need to research to find out what keywords you need to use. It gives you an idea about the relevant terms that people search for, so you know what people search for when looking for the products you are affiliated with, and then use those keywords to help them find your page or website. For instance, when you are typing something in a search engine like Google, you will notice that the search engine also suggests something before you have even finished typing. At least half of the time, what you are searching for shows up. Google calls it Google Suggest. You can also use Google Insight or Adwords Keyword Estimator to get an idea about the keywords that people search for. In Black Hat SEO, people just research and find out the keywords that people search for and stuff their pages with them, but the same technique of researching can be used in an ethical way and for your own benefit. You can include this in your research to learn more about how people look for things, what terms they type, when looking for a business like yours, and then include them in your keywords. Because the end goal here is that the user should be able to find your website or page.

The keywords that you use on your page should not be too generic. If they are too generic, your page will get lost in the results. People looking for it will not find it easily, and the ranking will go down. If your business is about a weight loss product, then the keyword 'weight,' or 'loss,' will be too generic. The word weight will result in different articles, website, blogs, products, etc. about weight, while the term loss will lead to hundreds of pages about losses of different kinds.

Do not be too specific with your keywords either. Your goal is to increase the overall scope while staying on the topic. If your keywords are 'how to,' or similar, then websites like Wikihow and

HowThingsWork will take the lead, and your website will be lost in the results. The keywords need to be balanced so while the scope is broad, the results still lead to your website.

The process of ranking higher in search results takes time. The keywords you use should be consistent with what your website is about. You have to stay focused and approach the same thing in different ways. The keywords should not be about something that you focus on once in a while only. If your keywords are focussed on what you do regularly, are consistent, then voila! Your website will rank higher! Whatever your website focuses on, whatever your keywords are, write about them as often as you can.

Try not to keep the keywords limited to the general writing. The titles should always include a keyword or two. Keep the titles short but make sure that there is a sprinkling of keywords in them. Ideally, a title should be between 10-14 words, and should start with a keyword. Subtitles can also be utilised for keywords; you can use more keywords in the subtitles. The description is where the rest of the content is. An ideal density of keywords is said to be 1%, which means that there should ideally be at least one keyword in every 100 words of description or content. For better search engine optimisation, make sure that the keywords are used in the first 3 lines, or the introductory lines, of the page.

Try to build links. Get similar and relevant websites to link back to your website or pages. If the content on your website is good enough, people will automatically link back to it. If you write a good article on giving a back massage, someone writing about getting rid of back pain and suggesting massage may link back to your page. Similarly, if you offer a good hair product, a website that contains information about hair may link back to your page to let people know that the product you offer is good. Alternatively, you can bring attention to your page. You can ask people to link back to your page, not only for building links but also to help others.

Chapter 5 – Fifth Step – Choosing an Affiliate Program

Before you decide on an affiliate program, you need to consider a few things first, like what the potential for selling products in a certain niche is. Since you will be promoting those products on your website or blog, you need to go for something that you actually have an interest in. Do not just opt for the first offer you get or whatever pays the highest profits, because you will have to do your part in selling those products too. You will have to write about those products, tell people their benefits, different ways they can use those products in, etc. and you can't do any of that until you have an interest in that product. If the product interests and excites you, go for it. And if it doesn't catch your interest, forget it.

Select a Niche

You will have to select a certain niche. As discussed in the beginning, we want to keep our blog or website to affiliate with more than one programs instead of a certain product, but we will be selecting a particular niche. If you are interested in health, you can select that niche. You can do your research and write about health to bring health-conscious people to your blog, while simultaneously promoting those products. The health niche will allow you to get affiliated with a wide variety of products like weight loss solutions, weight gain solutions, hair products, herbal products, skin products, organic products, etc. Your niche defines your blog or website and the products you promote.

Stay Relevant

If you have a health blog, do not try to sell sewing machines. The people who will frequent your blog will trust you as an expert in the selected niche, like health, so you have to promote products that are relevant to that niche. If you want to promote and sell things, go for things that 'your visitors' will actually have an interest in. If they are visiting your blog for health, they certainly won't have any interest in a sewing machine. Stay relevant to keep the potential buyers interested. You can also use Google Trends; it will help you analyse the potential products you want to sell.

Chapter 6 – Sixth Step – Selecting Products

There are two main types of products available in affiliate programs. The products are either digital or physical. You have to see which type of products are going to bring you more profits, a digital ebook or a physical supplement? There are pros and cons associated with each, but generally the digital products are preferred.

With digital products there is no hassle. For instance, if you are promoting an ebook on health, all the buyer will have to do is download it, simple as that. This makes it simple, convenient, fast, and hassle free for everyone. While with physical products, there is shipping, delivery, handling, and there can be return issues as well. There is more room for profits in digital products as well, chiefly because they never run out of stock. In physical products, you could get a customer and lose him in an instant if the product is not in stock.

You can start your affiliate marketing by signing up on an affiliating marketing website. The good thing about these websites is that they already have a lot of products and they allow you to choose the ones you want to promote. There is more room for promotions and greater margin for profits associated with them as well. Moreover, most affiliate marketing websites also handle the payments, so you do not have to wait for the business or website owner to send the payment to you. An affiliate marketing website will pay you regularly, as per their own regulations, so you do not have to worry about delays in payments or similar issues.

When selecting products, go for something that is being promoted by more than 15-20 other people because this indicates that the product is selling well. You should not always go for the products that are the most expensive, instead you should go with products that sell more. If a product gives you more profit but hardly ever sells then opt for something that gives you less profit per sale but sells more. You should get an estimate on the sales of each product and compare the expected profits before deciding on the product to promote. Whichever products give you more profit, should be the one that you should promote. The products that are neither too expensive nor too cheap are the ones that sell the most.

Tip: You can start you affiliate marketing with ClickBank.

Chapter 7 – Seventh Step – Building a Database of Users/Customers

It is important to build a database of your users and customers. When you establish your credibility and your regular visitors start trusting you, you should cash on it. You can start email lists and ask your visitors to subscribe to them. You can start emailing them regularly, like once a week. When emailing your customers, you should not always try to sell products because that leads to the feeling of being forced to buy something. If you always try to sell them something, they will start unsubscribing.

You have to send them emails that will give them value. If your blog is about health, instead of always trying to force them to buy something, gain their trust and get them interested by sharing valuable information with them, like telling them about super foods, exercise programs, importance of eating vegetables, etc. And wherever you get a chance, you can add a product you want to promote as a suggestion in your email. The emphasis on value in emails is because emails are direct, personal, and private. They are between you and your subscriber or customer.

If you can offer some sort of incentive to your subscribers then that would be a huge plus. It tells your subscribes that you care about them, and gives them a reason to continue the subscription. People who fail to provide value in their emails or spam the inboxes of their subscribers usually end up with people unsubscribing from their lists. You need to ensure that you give the same value to your subscribers in emails that you give them on your website or blog. The quality should not be compromised at any cost.

Following are some things you need to remember when writing emails:

Subject

This is the first thing your subscribers will look at. If it is interesting, they will open the email up, otherwise they will ignore it.

Focus

You have to keep the email focussed. The content of the email should go with whatever was in the subject line. This part is about trust, and you do not want to mislead your subscribers.

Keep It Short

No one has time to read super long emails. You do not have to email entire articles to your subscribers. Keep things short and to the point, and try to keep the emails under 500 words. If you want them to read an article, add a link to it.

Proofread

Lastly, it is very important to proofread your emails. If your emails contain spelling mistakes and typos, lack structure, then you are telling your subscribers that you really don't care about them. In return, they will not care either. Your credibility would go down. The email should look like it is purposefully and carefully written by you. Do not make it look like you just wrote it to get a weight off your shoulders.

Conclusion

Thank you again for downloading this book!

I hope this book was able to help you to begin earning money through affiliate marketing.

The next step is to apply the information learned within this book and go out and make things happen. I know you can make this work for you!

Finally, if you enjoyed this book, please take the time to share your thoughts and post a review on Amazon. It'd be greatly appreciated!

Thank you and good luck!

eBay Business

9 Steps to Selling $60,000+ in Products Your First Year on eBay!

Table of Contents

Affiliate Marketing for Beginners 1
7 Steps to Earning $200+ in less than 25 Hours a Week 1
Table of Contents 2
eBay Business 17
9 Steps to Selling $60,000+ in Products Your First Year on eBay! 17

Introduction

I want to thank you and congratulate you for downloading the book, "eBay Business: 11 Simple Steps to selling $60,000 in Product Your First Year in Business!"

This book contains proven steps and strategies on how to start and grow an eBay business to the point of selling $60,000 worth of product within the first year of business. The information I will share with you in this book is exactly how I sold $60,000 in product my first year in business!

While being able to accomplish the same results as me is not guaranteed, as we all have different work ethics and time to dedicate to the business, but what I can assure you is that this book will help you to take your eBay business to the next level!

Many people underestimate the power of eBay and don't realize the income potential that lies within this amazing platform if performed correctly.

I myself and countless others I have had the privilege to meet have made eBay their full – time income and continue to live off the money received from the business on a daily basis! Right now eBay holds a gold mine of profits and the money is up for grabs! The only thing stopping people from getting there cut of the pie is the simple fact of getting started and becoming educated!

In this book I will show you how to get a piece of the action and if you are committed I will specifically share with you the strategies that helped me to earn over $60,000 in sales my first year in business!

Let's get started. Take my hand and let me lead you down the road to success!

Chapter 1 - My Story; How I Sold $60,000 in Product My First Year

Before I started my eBay business a few years back I was struggling to make ends meet in the car selling business.

I had two kids, a wife, a stack of bills and felt lost and confused. My company was slowly going downhill, jobs were being cut, and I knew it was only a matter of time until I lost my job.

To make a long story short, a few months later, I lost my job.

I was devastated and had to think very quickly how I was going to support my family.

After spending countless hours surfing the web I decided I was going to start an eBay business.

The only question was, how was I going to get started, what was I going to sell, where was I going to get product, and how would I make enough money to support my family.

So you're probably thinking, "how in the hell did you figure all that out".

Well, let me tell you what I did, I STUDIED MY ASS OFF!

I read every article ever published, I trolled eBay blogs, I watched YouTube videos, I spoke to others in the business, I went to conferences, and attended local eBay seminars.

I became 100% committed to learning everything I could in regards to building a profitable eBay business!

And let me tell you; it paid off!

A year later I had sold over $60,000 in products my first year and made enough profits to support my family, pay the bills, and live a comfortable life.

With that being said I want to share with you the steps and strategies I took to make this happen.

If you are ready to start making some real money by starting an eBay business then continue reading, you won't regret it!

Chapter 2- Step 1: Creating a Vision for your eBay Business

The first thing I did before I started taking massive action in my eBay business was to create a vision for my business.

If you take a look at any successful business that was ever started you will soon realize it ALWAYS STARTED WITH A VISION.

Someone took the time to draw up the plans and create the vision that would one day be realized.

Without a vision you will never be able to create anything great, this is a key determinant in your success.

In order to create a vision you must take the time to figure out where you currently are today and where you want to go.

Ask yourself these questions:

- What kind of business do I want to create?
- Why do I want to create a business?
- How much money do I want to create in my business
- How will I feel once I create this business?
- How many employees will I have in my business or will it be soley operated.

  Will not all of the questions you ask yourself have to be defined exactly this moment; it would be smart to begin to create a compelling vision for what you want to create by the end of the year.

For me personally my vision was to create a business that was sustainable over the long term. I wanted to create a business that made over $60,000 in gross sales the first year and would provide me with enough money to support my family. I knew that if I created this business I would feel amazing. I also envisioned having at least 2 people helping me to run the business once all was said and done. So this was my vision.

Have you created your vision?

If not, take the time now and create the vision!

If you want to go above and beyond one thing that I did in addition was to create a vision board. This helped a ton!

Pretty much what I did was I took a big piece of cardboard and glued pictures of images that would resonate with the accomplishment of my vision.

Every morning when I woke I would look at my vision board and would be reminded of my goal.

This was a driving force in my success.

Create a vision now!

Chapter 3- Step 2: Purchasing Equipment and Supplies

Purchasing the right type of equipment for your eBay business will be an important factor in determining the levels of success you endure.

By purchasing the right type of equipment you will better your chances of selling your items on eBay for top dollar, will save time and become more efficient and overall, and will better your chances of making money over the long haul.

Recommended Equipment

- Camera or high end cell phone
- Backdrop or light box
- Lighting Kit
- Laser Printer
- Computer or Laptop
- Adhesive labels

- Cardboard boxes or Free USPS boxes
- Poly Bags and Poly Mailers
- Tape
- Thank you stickers for all eBay purchases
- Cleaning products such as simple green
- Storage Boxes for inventory
- Masking Tape to track inventory on boxes

Listed above were some of the basic items you will need to get you started on your path towards selling $60,000 in product your first year on eBay! Of course, this is just a basic list, and your list may include more or less depending on the type of items you sell, but for now, this should cover you pretty well.

If you decide to start selling items such as clothing, it may be smart to go above and beyond and purchase a mannequin, clothing racks, clothing hangers, a steamer, and equipment like this that tailors to your specific needs.

Chapter 4- Step 3: Putting Together Your Office Space

The next step you must take is to begin putting together your office space.

I know this step will differ for everyone depending on the amount of space you have; but you will need to do your best to create a dedicated space for your eBay business.

Luckily for me I had a spare bedroom in our house which I was able to dedicate to my office, but for you, that may be the basement, attic, a den, or even the garage.

The main reason you will need to put together an office space is because you will need a territory to be able to organize inventory, list items, ship items, and handle customer service issues via your computer.

I have seen other's get away with not having a committed office space but it is extremely difficult to stay organized.

Trust me, once you begin to really scale up your business things will get hectic, and being able to find certain things when you need it will save you a ton of time!

If you have the money, and aren't tapped out of funds, a great alternative is to rent out a small office space or storage locker.

While a storage locker typically won't allow you to set up a computer or have access to electrical outlets, it will give you extra space to store inventory in the case your space is limited at home.

An office space would be the best because it would allow you to have everything you need in one space, would eliminate distractions, and would keep you the most organized.

Whatever your personal situation is you need to be sure you create an office space for your business.

This will be a strong foundation for you to build upon.

Now that you have set up your office space let's move on to the next step!Chapter 5- Step 4: Setting up your eBay and PayPal Account

Now that you have decided to launch your business on eBay, the first thing you will need to do is create an eBay seller account. Creating an eBay account is very easy and can be completed in 5 simple steps.

Step 1: Go to www.ebay.com

At this point you will look for the *Register new account* tab; it should be located towards the top of the page.

Step 2: Register for an eBay seller account

At this stage you will be asked to create a new user ID and password, and enter a valid email and home address. In addition you will need to verify your phone number and specify an automatic payment method for paying seller fees, and for handling reimbursement charges.

Step 3: This step may not apply to everybody, but if you previously provided an anonymous email service such as a yahoo, Gmail or Outlook account on the eBay registration page, you will be redirected to another page that requires additional information for authenticating your identity. This authentication process is pretty straight forward and will typically involve you providing a valid credit or debit card.

Step 4: You will be asked to log into the email account you associated with your eBay account to confirm your account. This should activate your account.

Step 5: Continue to the account settings tab and **create** a new PayPal account. If you already have a PayPal account then you can link your existing PayPal account to the new eBay account you have created instead.

Why Do You Need A PayPal Account?

A PayPal account will allow you to receive money for the items you sell on eBay. In addition, it will enable you to send and request money transfers worldwide. PayPal is a highly secure service and is committed to protect your personal and credit card information, including using automatic encryption for all transmitted data.

After visiting PayPal's website you will see that there are different types of PayPal accounts, and you may be wondering which type of account you should choose. Below I will go into more detail about the different PayPal accounts available, and show you which should be the most beneficial to you.

Choosing the Right Type of PayPal Account

There are three types of PayPal accounts you will have the option to choose from once you are ready to sign up for PayPal. The three choices are Personal, Premier and Business. In my opinion, there is only one PayPal account I would suggest getting for the time being, but for now, follow along as I explain the different types. Having an understanding of the accounts will benefit you in the long run as your business grows and expands!

Since your primary purpose for a PayPal account will be for selling merchandise on eBay, you will want to avoid signing up for a Personal account. This is because the Personal PayPal account is geared more towards eBay *buyers* who are looking to *shop* and pay online. The major reason the Personal account will not work as well for you as an eBay seller is that it will not allow you to accept all forms of payment as seller.These forms of payments include some credit cards, debit cards and bank account payments. In addition, the Personal PayPal account will limit the volume of credit and debit card transactions you can perform per year, which will inhibit your eBay business greatly when you start to make consistent sales.

Signing up for a Premier PayPal account will give you the ability to accept all forms of payments and will also grant you an unlimited amount of transactions per year. The Premier PayPal account is probably the most common account seller's sign up for when getting started to sell on eBay.

The last account option is the PayPal Business account. The Premier and Business PayPal accounts are very similar and only have a few slight differences. First off, the Business account would work best for the owner of an established eBay business operating on a much larger scale, and who wants to conduct business under an official company or group name (this will require having tax id #). Secondly, the Business PayPal account allows access to special auction tools, downloadable Log and limited employee access to account information.

Based on the features of the different accounts, I would recommend getting a Premier PayPal account initially and then upgrading to a Business account down the road if necessary. And now, it is time for you to sign up for a PayPal account.

You are getting even closer to getting your very own eBay business started.

Congratulations, you are now all set up to start selling on eBay! At this point I am sure you are very excited to start looking for products to purchase and can hardly wait to start rolling in the profits!

Are you ready to learn how you can begin sourcing profitable products to sell on eBay? If so, let's jump to the next chapter!

Chapter 6- Step 5: Sourcing Inventory

When it comes to making a ton of money from your eBay business one of the key factors in doing so is having the ability to source profitable inventory.

While there may be a ton more of ideas out there for how you can source inventory, the ideas I share with you below are the one's which have worked best for me.

With that being said, try each out for yourself, see what works best, and go from there!

Thrift Stores

Sourcing inventory from thrift stores is probably my favorite way to acquire super awesome inventory that can make me a lot of money on eBay. Where I live I am literally surrounded by thrift stores that are offering cheap clothing inventory on a regular basis. Having a large amount of thrift stores in your area can be a great opportunity for you! A quick tip for getting cheap inventory at thrift stores is to go on the half off days. Many thrift stores will dedicate a day to a special discount, or slashed rate, to keep their inventory moving. This is when you need to pounce on the opportunity and get your items dirt cheap!

Yard Sales or Tag Sales

If you live in a pretty populated area; yard sales or otherwise known as tag sales on the east coast is a terrific way to find profitable inventory for your business. I have found Saturday's to be the best day to go to yard sales in terms of finding the best inventory. Make sure if you really want to have a good experience that you plan out a route in advance the night before and you wake up early. As the saying goes, "The early bird get's the worm". This is one of the best methods for acquiring quality inventory on a budget!

Auctions

Personally I rarely ever go to auctions due to the abundance of thrift stores and yard sales I have locally in my general area, but I know of many who love auctions and do very well. In my opinion inventory at auctions will typically be more expensive, and the competition will be higher, but if you have a specialized niche you are very educated in you can do extremely well.

Flea Markets

Flea markets can be very lucrative if you again have specialized knowledge in one or more niche areas. I have a friend who specialized in antiques and makes an absolute killing every weekend! Again, just like the auctions, I rarely use this method due to my area and specialized expertise, but like I said my friend and many other's love this method and you can find some great stuff to resell on eBay!

Craigslist

Craigslist is probably my 3rd favorite method for acquiring quality inventory to resell on eBay. Many people underestimate the power of craigslist and don't think that there is anything on this site besides garbage, but I am telling you right now they are dead wrong! When I first got started reselling items on eBay, craigslist was the avenue I focused on the most. I was selling over $3,000 a month of furniture alone by purchasing off craigslist and selling on eBay via local pick-up. Craigslist is a great method to look into!

Chapter 7 -Step 6: Listing Products on eBay

When it comes to listing products on eBay this is where you will make your money.

Many people struggle with listing products on eBay and tend to fail at executing this step.

The reason people find this step so difficult is because of its dry to the bone nature. To be honest, there is nothing sexy about sitting down at a computer for 3-4 hours a night listing products. This task can be very repetitive, boring, and can definitely feel daunting at times!

What most people succeed at is sourcing inventory because of the adrenaline rush. There is nothing more fun than going to a thrift store on a Sunday morning searching for the next profitable item.

With that being said, we most hold ourselves accountable and commit ourselves to listing on a daily basis if we want to accomplish our goals and truly fulfill our vision.

The topic of listing products on eBay is extremely broad and could take hours and hours to cover so instead I will list 10 tips below for improving the process of listing products on eBay.

1.) Create a listing routine

Having a listing routine will be crucial to your success.

Sit down right now and set a time each day you will commit yourself to listing products on eBay.

Also write down how many items you plan on listing. Make sure you do what you set forth to do and eliminate all distractions!

2.) Create a template for description

A template for your description will allow you to save time in the long run. If you are selling a lot of similar items you can create a template in word that contains product information, return policy, shipping turnaround, and anything else that would remain consistent in all your listings. Create a template, save it in word, and copy and paste it into all of your listings when listing products on eBay to save time and assure you cover all of your bases!

3.) Use good keywords

Using good keywords in your listing is super important for potential customers to find your products for sale. The main place in your listing you will want to focus your keywords are in the title. You can use a free tool called the Google keyword planner which will allow you to discover what the best keywords are that you should use for each specific item you are selling. Check it out!

4.) Make your best picture the main picture

You will want to make sure that the picture that best depicts your item is shown for your thumbnail. Remember most potential customers will not click on your listing unless they are intrigued by the main picture. Keep this in mind at all times!

5.) Experiment with buy and now and auction formats

Depending on the items you decide to sell you may want to focus more heavily on buy it now or auction style listings. In order to discover which is best for your items you will want to experiment. Take some time to do some A/B testing to see what listing format yields the best results for you. Personally for myself I enjoy using buy it now, 30 days, with a best offer for my items.

6.) Offer free shipping

In today's day of age people are looking for free shipping. Now if you are selling items that are extremely big and heavy this may not apply to you, as it wouldn't be smart to offer free shipping, but for most items you can build the shipping price into the list price.

Offering free shipping will not only help you to attract more customers but it will also help you to rank higher in the eBay search engine as eBay favors sellers who offer free shipping. In addition free shipping will help you to become a top rated seller which will save you money.

7.) Offer 1 day shipping turn around

It is a must that you offer 1 day shipping turn around if you want to build a profitable eBay business. Customers want their items fast and will not buy from sellers who take their sweet time shipping!

8.) Always include more than enough information about the product

This is something I see many sellers failing to do and I find it really kills there results. You need to remember when people are shopping online they are relying on the information you put forth in the listing. Yes if they have a question they can send you an email, but most won't. Give your potential customers all the necessary information they will need right then and there on the spot to make a buying decision. This alone will make a huge difference in your eBay business!

9.) Always fill out the item specifics

The information you put into the item specifics actually has a purpose. What this section does is communicate with the eBay search engine. The more information you fill out in the item specifics the more times your listing will pop up when customers are searching for relative information. Never skip this part!

10.) Accept returns

Returns are a most if you want to be successful on eBay. Even the big box stores like Walmart and Toys R us have to deal with returns. While it stinks to take back a return, it's just part of the business. If you fail to accept returns you will lose out on a lot of business. Remember most people will not return an item. For me my return rate is typically less than 2%. Accept returns it makes you look professional!

Chapter 8- Step 7: Shipping Products on eBay

5 Factors to Consider Before You Ship an Item

The Weight of the Item

The weight of the item you are going to be shipping will play a huge role in determining how to ship it most efficiently. Typically, the heavier the shipment, the more expensive it will be to ship. With that in mind, you should choose a shipment method carefully before you list an item, or your shipping costs could end up being higher than you originally thought they would be. Coming up, I will teach you about a method that will keep your shipping costs way down regardless of the weight!

Location of Shipment

Generally, the farther away an item needs to be shipped, the more expensive it will be to ship it. If you live on the West Coast or the East Coast, you need to pay particular attention when shipping to the opposite side of the country—the price can add up quickly regardless of the weight. If this is the case for you, don't worry. I've got some tips that will keep your shipping costs down and allow you to stay profitable when on eBay!

Size of the Item

The size of an item you are shipping can play a key role in determining how you are going to ship the item. Some items will have to go into a certain box because of the size.

Price Point (How Expensive the Item Is)

The reason you need to consider the price is because certain shipping methods are riskier than are others. What I mean by risky is that depending on how you choose to ship your item, you may have a greater chance of encountering problems. For example, I have found that packages shipped standard post (the USPS method that used to be called parcel post) tend to get mistreated and broken more often than those shipped priority mail. The reason I believe this happens is because standard post, as a less expensive alternative, takes longer to arrive at its destination and therefore passes through more hands along the way. With priority shipping, packages tend to be treated more carefully due to the premium paid and ultimately fewer hands touching the package on its way to the destination, which decreases risk of a problem. If you are shipping a valuable item that sold for a lot of money, it may be wise to pay a little extra to assure the item is handled with respect while in transit and arrives to your customer intact and in good condition.

International

When you ship internationally, you will still consider the factors you consider while shipping domestically, such as weight, location, size, and price point. However, you need to be especially careful because postage rates are so high for international shipments and you can get burned quickly. In addition, a few things are different when it comes to international versus domestic shipping. In the next section, I will touch on those differences and a few other concerns of which you should be aware when shipping internationally.

Methods for Shipping

Before I talk about the various methods of shipping, I want to give you a quick tip that I hope you are already practicing. What I want to talk about is printing out your postage from home. If you are unaware of what this is, it's purchasing your postage online instead of buying it in person at the post office. The reason I suggest you do this is because, first of all, it will save you tons of time at the post office. Secondly, purchasing the actual postage online will save you money. I'm not going to get into this topic too much right now because you can easily learn more about it by doing a simple Google search, but just know that if you are currently not purchasing your postage online from home, then it is something you need to start looking more into.

In the section following, I will give you the best methods and go into more detail when items on eBay. As a disclaimer, I want to mention that the rates and methods of shipment I talk about below are subject to change by the United States Postal Service, and policies and methods may be different depending upon when you are reading this content. In addition, especially when it comes to the legal flat rate envelopes, many post offices are not accepting items to be shipped if the packages are overly stuffed. This is also true when it comes to the flat rate boxes provided by the USPS. Please be sure to read the fine print at the time of shipping when using any of the methods to assure you are obeying the USPS rules of conduct. Below I will provide a picture of the shipping method, reasons for why you should or shouldn't use the method, price to ship, and a few other bits of information I feel you may find helpful.

Legal Flat Rate Envelope

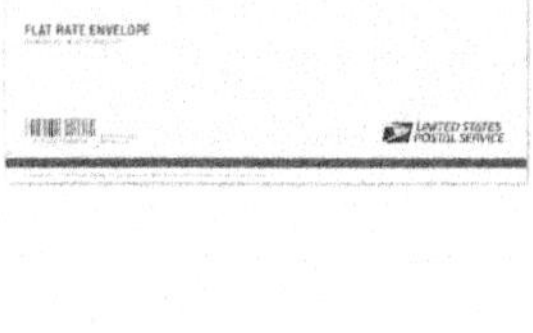

Price to Ship: $4.99 online

Size: 9.5x15 inches

Pros of Using This Method: Flat rate cost anywhere in the country regardless of weight, fast shipping, cheapest method possible to ship

Cons of Using This Method: May be hard to fit item inside, decreased protection with envelope

Be Aware: Some post offices frown on people using the legal flat rate envelopes to ship items other than documents. Be careful when overstuffing and overdoing it with tape.

Where to Purchase: Free on the USPS website

Bubble Mailer Flat Rate

Price to Ship: $5.35 online

Size: 9.5x 12.5 inches

Pros of Using This Method: Added protection over the legal flat rate envelope, flat rate cost anywhere in the country regardless of weight, very cheap to ship, fast shipping with priority

Cons of Using This Method: Will only be able to fit an extremely small blazer or sport coat

Be Aware: You may have difficulty fitting item inside. By jamming the item inside too much, you are risking having the item damaged during shipment.

Where to Purchase: Free on the USPS website

Medium Flat Rate Box (2 Choices)

Box # 1

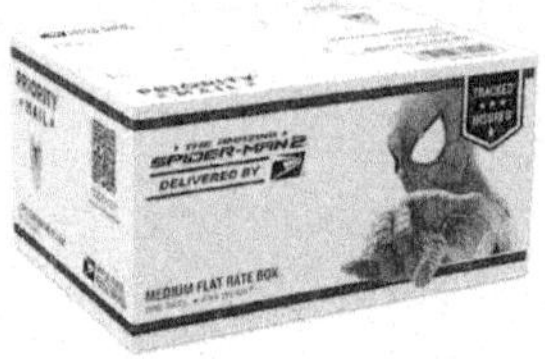

Price to Ship: $10.65 online

Size: 11 x 8.5 x 5.5 inches

Pros of Using This Method: Flat rate cost anywhere in the country regardless of weight, can fit most items for less than $11.00, box protects items very well, fast shipping with priority

Cons of Using This Method: Flat rate postage can be more expensive than other methods if you are shipping to a nearby state

Be Aware: The box must not be overly stuffed or bulging out. The post office will give you a hard time if the content does not fit nicely inside.

Where to Purchase: Free on the USPS website

Box # 2

Price to Ship: $10.65 online

Size: 11-7/8x 3-3/8 x 13-5/8inches

Pros of Using This Method: Flat rate cost anywhere in the country regardless of weight, can fit nearly any item for less than $11.00, box protects items very well, fast shipping with priority

Cons of Using This Method: Flat rate postage can be more expensive than other methods if you are shipping to a nearby state, medium flat rate box #2 can be more difficult to fit thicker items

Be Aware: The box must not be overly stuffed or bulging out. The post office will give you a hard time if the content does not fit nicely inside.

Where to Purchase: Free on the USPS website

Large Flat Rate Box

Price to Ship: $14.80 online

Size: 12 x 12 x 5.5 inches

Pros of Using This Method: Flat rate cost anywhere in the country regardless of weight, can fit most items for less than $15.00, box protects items very well, fast shipping with priority

Cons of Using This Method: Cost to ship using this method may eat a lot of your profit; a cheaper alternative is usually available

Be Aware: The box must not be overly stuffed or bulging out. The post office will give you a hard time if the content does not fit nicely inside.

Where to Purchase: Free on the USPS website

Plain Box (Priority)

Price to Ship: Depends on location and weight

Size: Any size. Beware of very large boxes, as you can be hit with an oversize fee. Also larger boxes weigh more and will make shipment more expensive.

Weight Limit: None

Pros of Using This Method: Can use any size box (keeping in mind oversize fees), can purchase extra-strong boxes for added protection

Cons of Using This Method: Can be more expensive versus using flat rate boxes, may have to pay for boxes if you cannot get them for free

Be Aware: The price will vary according to weight and location.

Where to Purchase: You can easily get boxes for free if you ask stores, U-Line, Wal-Mart

Standard Post (Formerly Parcel Post)

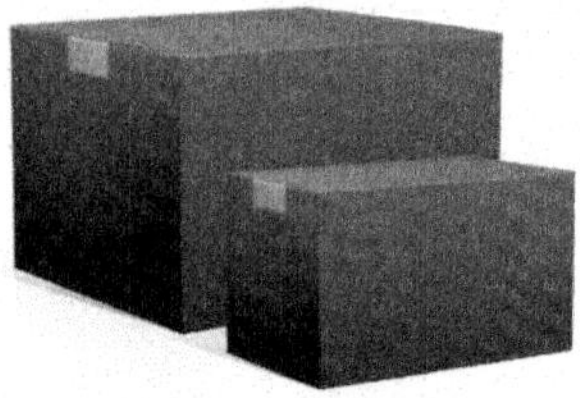

Price to Ship: Depends on the weight and location

Size: Can use any size box you like

Pros of Using This Method: Can be a cheaper alternative for shipping very heavy items (for example, if shipping a lot of five suits across the country)

Cons of Using This Method: Very slow shipping, better chance of items getting damaged due to increased transit time, can be more expensive than priority depending on location

Be Aware: Very slow shipping. You need to use a plain box; you cannot ship parcel using a priority box. Go above and beyond to protect your items very well when shipping this method.

Where to Purchase: You can easily get boxes for free if you ask stores, Wal-Mart, U-Line

Regional Rate Boxes

(4 Recommended Choices)

Regional Box A1

Price to Ship: Depends on location

Size: 10 x 7 x 4.75 inches

Weight Limit: 15 pounds

Pros of Using This Method: Ships at a 2-pound rate and can save you money depending on weight and location of shipment, priority mail is very fast shipping, box offers excellent protection for item

Cons of Using This Method: It may be cheaper to ship in flat rate envelope if item fits into one

Be Aware: Price differs by location. There is a weight limit .You must print postage online.

Where to Purchase: Free on the USPS website

Regional Box A2

Price to Ship: Depends on location

Size: 10-15/16 x 2-3/8 x 12-13/16 inches

Weight Limit: 15 pounds

Pros of Using This Method: Ships at a 2-pound rate and can save you money depending on weight and location of shipment, priority mail is very fast shipping, box offers excellent protection for item

Cons of Using This Method: It may be cheaper to ship in flat rate envelope if item fits into one

Be Aware: Price differs by location. There is a weight limit. You must print postage online.

Where to Purchase: Free on the USPS website

Regional Box B1

Price to Ship: Depends on location

Size: 12 x 10.25 x 5 inches

Weight Limit: 20 pounds

Pros of Using This Method: Ships at a 4-pound rate and can save you money depending on weight and location of shipment, priority mail is very fast shipping, box offers excellent protection for item

Cons of Using This Method: More expensive than Regional A boxes

Be Aware: Price differs by location. There is a weight limit. You must print postage online.

Where to Purchase: Free on the USPS website

Regional Box B2

Price to Ship: Depends on location

Size: 14-3/8 x 2-7/8 x 15-7/8 inches

Weight Limit: 20 pounds

Pros of Using This Method: Ships at a 4-pound rate and can save you money depending on weight and location of shipment, priority mail is very fast shipping, box offers excellent protection for item

Cons of Using This Method: More expensive than Regional A boxes

Be Aware: Price differs by location. There is a weight limit. You must print postage online.

Where to Purchase: Free on the USPS website

International Shipping

When it comes to shipping your items internationally, most of the same rules apply as if you were shipping domestically, but there are a few things you will want to be aware of.

One of the main things you will want to know about shipping internationally is that anything less than 4 pounds is eligible to be shipped via first class mail international. This differs from domestic shipping, in which you can only ship first class mail if the item weighs 13 ounces or less. When shipping domestically, first class mail will not be an option because all blazers, sport coats, and suits will weigh more than 13 ounces.

First class mail international does have its drawbacks. Some of the issues you may be concerned about are slow shipping times and the lack of tracking. I have found that when shipping first class mail international, the chances of running into a problem—such as buyers claiming they did not receive their items—is greatly increased in comparison to shipping priority international. As a side note, when shipping first class mail, or even priority, perform due diligence when deciding to ship to certain countries. As an example, I have found to have many problems shipping internationally to countries such as Brazil, Russia and Italy. Ship with caution!

How to Ship First Class Mail International

When shipping first class international you will have two main options. From my experience I have found it best to use either a large poly bag or a plain cardboard box. You have to keep in mind the weight limit, so make sure the item and materials weigh less than 4 pounds!

Option #1

Poly Bag

Price to Ship: Depends on location and weight

Size: I like to use 12x15inches or bigger

Weight Limit: Less than 4 pounds

Pros of Using This Method: Poly bag is very lightweight, using poly bags to ship first class mail versus priority will save you money

Cons of Using This Method: Less protection using a poly bag versus a box, first class mail is slower, no tracking included.

Be Aware: Shipments may take months to arrive at destination. You may want to purchase insurance from a company. I use ShipSaver through eBay to insure packages. Only certain countries are eligible for insurance internationally. I want you to know that if a package does not arrive at a destination, eBay and PayPal will likely side with buyer and you will lose your money 99 percent of the time. With that in mind, definitely protect yourself by ordering insurance!

Where to Purchase: eBay or Amazon

Option #2

Plain Box

Price to Ship: Depends on location and weight

Size: Any size. Beware of super large boxes, as you can be hit with an oversize fee. Larger boxes weigh more, and you need to keep weight under 4 pounds to ship first class international.

Weight Limit: Less than 4 pounds

Pros of Using This Method: More protection versus poly bag

Cons of Using This Method: Using the box will be heavier and may be difficult to keep overall weight under 4 pounds

Be Aware: Shipments may take months to arrive at destination. You may want to purchase insurance from a company. I use Ship Saver through eBay to insure packages. Only certain countries are eligible for insurance internationally.

Where to Purchase: Get free from stores, U-Line, Wal-Mart

How to Ship Priority Mail International

When shipping priority mail international you can use all the methods I outlined for shipping domestically, except for the Regional Rate boxes. When using the flat rate boxes internationally, the costs can add up rather quickly. For that reason alone there are only a few methods I use on a consistent basis when shipping priority mail international because of the high cost. Overall, I try to use first class mail international as much as possible! Below I will mention a few of my favorite methods for shipping priority mail international.

Legal Flat Rate Envelope

Price to Ship: Depends on location

Size: 9.5x15 inches

Pros of Using This Method: Flat rate cost can save you a lot of money

Cons of Using This Method: May be hard to fit item inside, decreased protection with envelope

Be Aware: Some post offices frown on people using the legal flat rate envelopes to ship items other than documents. Be careful when overstuffing and overdoing it with tape.

Where to Purchase: Free on the USPS website

Plain Box (Priority Mail International)

Price to Ship: Depends on location and weight

Size: Any size. Beware of super large boxes, as you can be hit with an oversize fee. Also larger boxes weigh more and will make shipment more expensive.

Weight Limit: None

Pros of Using This Method: Can use any size box (keeping in mind oversize fees), can purchase extra-strong boxes for added protection

Cons of Using This Method: Can become quite expensive based on weight (try to use first class mail if you can, or use a legal flat rate envelope if the item will fit)

Be Aware: The price will vary according to weight and location.

Where to Purchase: Get free from stores, U-Line, Wal-Mart

Putting It All Together

Hopefully after reading through this chapter you have learned how to effectively ship your products on eBay

If you are new to shipping, I can guarantee you feel overwhelmed. But don't worry; it is normal and expected. Be sure to take your time when first beginning to ship your items, and please use this chapter as a reference to get you moving in the right direction. Before you know it, you will be moving much quicker and will be confident in your shipping abilities.

Honestly, now that you know what methods you can use to ship your products; it's all a matter of figuring out which method will be the cheapest and most effective for each individual item you ship. There are a lot of factors that can play a role when it comes to deciding how to ship an item, so do not rush your decision making. I congratulate you on getting through this chapter; you have now put yourself in a position to save tons of money throughout the future by learning how to ship like a pro!

Chapter 9: Step 8: Scaling the Business up & Creating Systems

Putting systems in place will make or break you when you are running an eBay business. You need to have a system in place for cleaning inventory, storing inventory, relisting items, editing pictures, listing items, managing employee (if you have one), shipping items, and the list goes on and on.

I am not going to go into major detail in terms of specific systems and how to create one, but I want to drill in your head why it is so important to have them.

Having systems in place for everything you do in your business will allow for things to run much more smoothly and will enable you to scale your business even bigger when the time is right.

If you want to figure out how to put the proper systems in place all you need to do is break down all of your daily tasks. Take a look at your method for storing your inventory and ask yourself, "Is this method efficient, can I improve this system anyway"? Doing this will give you some great ideas and will get your started on the right path to creating systems or better systems.

Trust me if you want to make $5,000 a month or more on eBay you will need systems in place!

As an example, one system I have in place has to do with my employee that works for me. What I do is I give my worker a stack of about 100 papers each Monday before he starts picturing the items that I will be listing each week. Each paper is known as a listing template and has the necessary information I would like him to fill out. By creating this system or otherwise known as a listing template it has allowed my employee to save time and become more efficient. This is an example of a system that saves time and saves me money!

Start thinking of how you can create

Scaling the business

If you want to sell $60,000 worth of products or more on eBay, your first year, it may be smart to hire an employee.

An employee can be great because it can allow you to delegate tasks off that are not required of you to do personally, and will allow you to free up time to spend on other more important projects.

When it comes to making money on eBay one of the greatest uses of your time will be out sourcing quality inventory.

While taking pictures, listing items, measuring items, cleaning items, shipping items, and so on it extremely important, in the big picture it does not make you money. In my opinion the money is made when you buy an item, and you need to spend as much time as possible looking for those items at thrift stores, auctions, yard sales, flea markets, and craigslist so you can make a ton of money in your eBay business.

So now that you know why you need an employee how in the world are you going to hire one? Well, from my personal experience I have hired a few friends, college students, retirees, and some random folks off of craigslist. So first thing I would suggest is talking to some friends and see if anyone is looking for some extra cash.

If you can't find any friends interested then I would look at the other options. Probably one of the easiest ways to do this would be to make a craigslist ad. In today's economy there are a ton of people looking for work and it is quite easy to find people. The key is finding good people that you can trust and do a good job. This will take some time!

A quick tip of advice when hiring people, try to only hire someone for a specific task. For example hire one person for taking pictures, another for listing items and another for sourcing items. I have found if you hire someone to do it all they will eventually leave you and do what you are doing their self!

Chapter 10: Step 9: How to be Success in your eBay business

Do you find yourself becoming stressed out because you are not achieving your eBay goals fast enough?

Maybe you see other's on eBay you getting the results you desire at lightning speed and can't figure out how they did it?

This can become quite frustrating and discouraging at times and it is totally understandable.

Trust me; I know firsthand exactly how you feel as I was in the same boat as you when I first got started on eBay.

But there is one thing I learned as time progressed...

Success takes time

No matter what you are looking to accomplish in life; I have come to realize that success will take time and there is a due process we must all go through.

Some people *may be a little faster, a tad bit quicker, or are slightly more gifted, naturally* – but in the end: ***time is always a factor we must all endure in realizing success***.

Below I will share some tips and tricks to keep in mind to better your chances of becoming successful on eBay.

Set realistic expectations

Many people, including myself at times, tend to set *unrealistic goals* or expectations in terms of what "we believe" we should accomplish in a given amount of time. Maybe we read a book that said we could make X amount of dollars in 30 days, or possibly we know a friend who started a business and quit his job in only 6 months and now lives on the beach in Hawaii.

Who knows what your story is, it will be different for us all, but regardless of what we have put into our head in terms of expectations we need to be sure they are "realistic". I'm a firm believer in being a **big dreamer** and think it's very healthy to set high goals for ourselves, but we need to actually believe we can do it.

Have you ever set a goal for yourself that you knew deep down inside ***you would never be able to accomplish?***

Maybe you set a goal for yourself that you would earn $10,000 on eBay within the first month of business only to realize you don't have the first clue how to make it happen?

Yes, that's called an ***unrealistic expectation*** and we all make them.

A better expectation would be to set a goal of $1,000 for the first month or something more "believable". This is important because it will allow us to better our chances of accomplishing our goals, will help us to build momentum, and we give us the strength we need to keep moving forward as we build bigger and bigger goals on our road towards success.

Model Success

Sometimes we try to reinvent the wheel hoping that we can shortcut the process and become successful faster. Many times this strategy backfires and actually causes us to accomplish our goals slower. There is no need to try to *"do things different"*, many people have done it before, and modeling success is one of the best methods for succeeding in a timely manner.

If you find yourself struggling to make things happen you may want to consider modeling someone who has succeeded already in your given field and begin to take action steps that they have already taken to become successful.

Become a Student

Failing to educate ourselves properly is one of the number one reasons why people fail to become successful.

If you study the people who are the most successful in life you will quickly notice they are students of whatever they have mastered.

It is important to consistently be learning, educating yourself, and absorbing information that could get you ahead of the game.

We are living in the information age and having knowledge is power. Become a student and watch your levels of success skyrocket in a much shorter period of time.

Stop doing what isn't working and do more of what is.

When I was first getting started on eBay I was selling many different types of items. After a while I noticed that items such as household products were taking too long to sell and weren't selling for that decent of a profit.

On the other hand I noticed that my clothing items were selling very quickly and for an excellent profit. From there on out I decided to focus more on selling clothing versus household items because of what I discovered.

In short I started to do more of what was working and stopped doing as much of what was not working.

This allowed me to speed up my path towards success on eBay and really helped me to grow my business!

Take a look at your current situation and see what you need to do more of and what you need to do less of. This will speed up your rate of success very fast.

Don't take shortcuts

If you want to accomplish your goals, dreams, and visions you need to put yourself in the mindset of *not taking shortcuts every chance you get.*

Quite often the daily tasks and common action steps we take to accomplish our goals is laying down a strong foundation for our future.

For example maybe you'd like to grow an Amazon business to $10,000 a month and attempt to shortcut success by avoiding how to learn the process of properly listing, photographing items, and pricing items because you want to hire an employee and scale the business faster.

While this may sound like a lucrative plan; what will you do when things go wrong? How will you fix a photography issue if you never learned photography yourself? How will you list your items when your employee becomes sick or Ill if you never learned yourself? While this example may be uncommon, the point I am trying to make is that a strong foundation is very important for anyone looking to succeed.

Be proactive

One of the most common reasons why people tend to never accomplish the levels of success they hope to endure, in a given amount of time, is because of the habit of **not being proactive.**

People love to complain, blame, make excuses, and come up with reasons for why they are not succeeding.

If you spend any amount of time around successful people you will realize they never fall into this trap.

Successful people are always being proactive, are positively thinking, and are working towards a solution.

Focus on the solution instead of the reason why you are not succeeding and you will move forward much quicker!

Take action everyday

This is probably the most important tip I can give you in this blog posting.

Take action everyday!

I have noticed that the people, who succeed most in life, in the quickest amount of time, are the *people who are constantly working towards their goals every day.*

The people who consistently fall short, and are considered to be unsuccessful are the **people who lack the habit of taking action every day.**

Small actions on a daily basis will add up to large results!

Consistency is key!

Keep your eye on the prize

Keeping your eye on the prize will be one of the leading motivators on your journey to become successful.

When times get tough and you don't feel like taking action; having that vision or prize in your mind will keep your moving.

When you are tired, low on sleep, and want to nap all day, having that end goal will keep you doing what you need to do to make things happen.

Constantly keeping your eye on the prize will give you the strength, endurance, and mental energy to keep striving in the direction of your dreams.

Never lose sight of your prize, always remind yourself as much as you can, and you will find yourself taking action every single day!

Enjoy the process

Learning to enjoy the process is something we all need to do if we want to become successful.

Sometime's the things we may need to do in order to succeed will be boring, bland, and not the most exciting thing in the world. But at the end of the day **we need to learn to enjoy the process.**

Take some time to take into consideration your daily routine and think of ways you can go about making it more enjoyable.

A few things I do to better enjoy my process is to play music, keep my workplace organized, eat healthy foods, take breaks to rejuvenate my mind, and exercise to get my blood flowing. For you it may be different, but think of ways you can enjoy the process, it will really help you to become more success in a faster amount of time!

Pay the price

At the end of the day you can follow all the tips and tricks I mentioned but if you are not willing to pay the price it will not mean anything.

Take some time now to think of your goals, think of where you are and where you want to be, think of the things you will need to do to become successful.

Once you do this, be willing to pay the price. Become committed, write down your goals, write down action steps you must take, and then pay the price.

Like Nike always said, **"Just do it"**

Conclusion

Thank you again for downloading this book!

I hope this book was able to help you to take your eBay business to the next level and really improve your life.

Remember it all starts with a vision, a plan and an inspired idea. From there it is up to you to take action on a daily basis until you reach your goal!

Keep educating yourself and never quit: I know you have what it takes to accomplish your eBay business dreams!

Finally, if you enjoyed this book, please take the time to share your thoughts and post a review on Amazon. It'd be greatly appreciated!

Thank you and good luck!

Bonus # 1: 27 Highly Profitable Items to sell on eBay

Affiliate Marketing for Beginners 1
7 Steps to Earning $200+ in less than 25 Hours a Week 1
Table of Contents 2
eBay Business 17
9 Steps to Selling $60,000+ in Products Your First Year on eBay! 17

Chapter 1: Handheld Electronics

Item# 1: *Nintendo Crystal Balloon Fight*

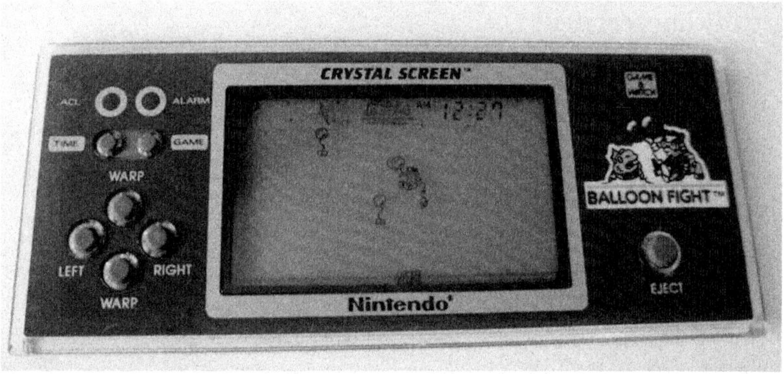

Average Resale: $400 - $600

Difficult To Find: Very Hard!

Final Note: Be sure to test the item first to make sure it works. Many of these handheld electronics will have defects which will affect the final resale value. Even with issues, I would still buy this item because it is so rare and will still bring in some decent money!

Item # 2: *Saitek Pro Bridge 311*

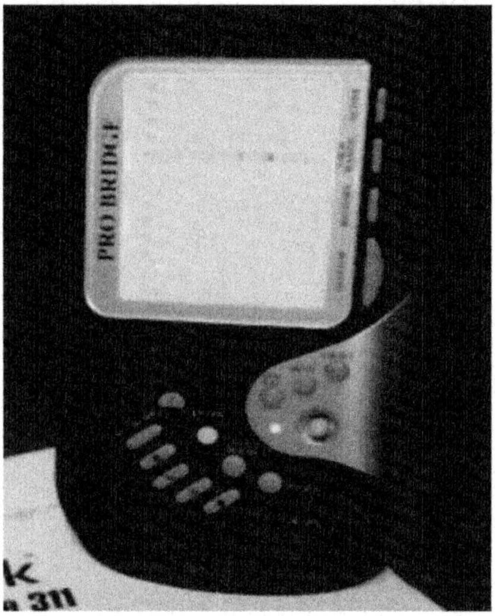

Average Resale: $100 - $300

Difficult To Find: Hard!

Final Note: These games are typically built very strong and tend to be working when I find them. Of course, even with that in mind, it is always smart to test hand held electronic games out first to make sure there are no major defects!

Item # 3: *Yahtzee*

Average Resale: $10-$25+

Difficult To Find: Easy - Medium

Final Note: These items are very abundant and used to bring in much more money but over the last few years the price has been declining. If you are to purchase this hand-held game please test first and purchase for very cheap (less than $3). The gold version is my favorite one to sell.

Chapter 2: Men's Clothing

Item# 4: *Ermenegildo Zegna Suit*

Average Resale: $100- $300+

Difficult To Find: Medium

Final Note: Ermenegildo Zegna is a very high end brand that can bring in some excellent profits. When inspecting this item before purchase make sure there are no stains, holes, or rips in lining (especially around the armpit area)

Item # 5: *Ralph Lauren "Big Pony" Polo Shirt*

Average Resale: $15-$40

Difficult To Find: Medium

Final Note: Ralph Lauren Polo is one of the easiest brands to sell of clothing on eBay. With that being said, some items do sell better than others within this brand. The big pony line is highly sought after and can bring some big money! Stick to the shirts that are bigger, vibrant in color, and are in good condition!

Item # 6: *Brooks Brothers Shorts*

Average Resale: $20-$40

Difficult To Find: Medium

Final Note: When it comes to buying and selling the Brooks Brothers shorts I like to stick to the ones that have an interesting theme on or the ones with an incredibly odd pattern. For example, I have sold a pair of Brooks Brothers shorts with a lobster theme on them for $30!

Chapter 3: Gaming Consoles

Item# 7: *Atari 2600*

Average Resale: $20-$50+

Difficult To Find: Medium

Final Note: When it comes to buying and selling the Atari 2600 make sure all accessories comes with the unit and if you can, test the unit. Many of these older units have issues, and if you discover one, if could mean the difference between a profit and a loss. The key to finding these units is to acquire the games and controllers with it. These sell best in bundles!

Item # 8: *Super Nintendo*

Average Resale: $30-$50+

Difficult To Find: Medium

Final Note: When it comes to buying and selling the Super Nintendo Console make sure all accessories comes with the unit and if you can, test the unit. Many of these older units have issues, and if you discover one, if could mean the difference between a profit and a loss. You will make the most money with these units if you acquire the games and controllers with it. These sell best in bundles!

Item # 9: *Nintendo 64*

Average Resale: $40-$60+

Difficult To Find: Medium

Final Note: **When it comes to buying and selling the Nintendo 64 systems make sure all accessories comes with the unit, and if you can, test the unit. Many of these older units have issues, and if you discover one, if could mean the difference between a profit and a loss. When dealing with these units try to find the ones that have a theme such as Pokémon, or are colored, like the one in the picture. They consoles will sell for a lot more money!Chapter 4: Blenders**

Item# 10: *Vitamix*

Average Resale: $100- $300+

Difficult To Find: Medium- Hard

Final Note: The more modern versions of the vitamix blender will bring in the most money. With that being said, the vintage one's that are stainless steel are not in as high of demand but can still bring in upwards to $100-$150. Also be on the lookout for any accessories that go along with the blender because they can bring in some great cash!

Item # 11: *Blendtec*

Average Resale: $150- $250+

Difficult To Find: Hard

Final Note: Besides the vitamix blender, the blendtec is probably the second most profitable blender you can find while sourcing at thrift stores, garage sales and flea markets. Like the vitamix, any accessories that go along with the blender can bring in some great cash! If you can, test this machine beforehand because I have had trouble in the past with the screen not turning on properly.

Item # 12: *Margaritaville*

Average Resale: $75- $200

Difficult To Find: Easy - Medium

Final Note: While the margaritaville blender is not nearly as popular, and in demand as the vitamix or the blendtec, this blender can bring in some good profits on eBay and is a lot easier to find! Make sure all the accessories come with the blender or the value will be beaten down greatly!

Chapter 5: Baseball Equipment

Item# 13: *Mizuno Baseball Gloves*

Average Resale: $25- $200+

Difficult To Find: Easy - Medium

Final Note: The prices can range greatly on any baseball glove depending on the condition, age, style and model. As a general rule of thumb the more fancy the glove looks the more money it will bring. A few things to look for are the quality of leather, laces and pocket. Also the first basemen and catchers gloves seem to yield higher profits!

Item # 14: *Redline Baseball Bats*

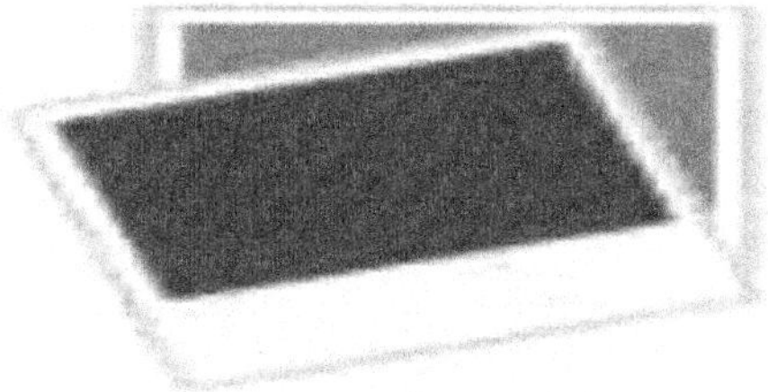

Average Resale: $75- $200+

Difficult To Find: Medium

Final Note: The prices can range greatly for these baseball bats depending on the size, weight, and condition. Make sure there are no cracks in the bat as this will be a deal breaker. Also be sure the grip is intact, and is not destroyed, or you may want to invest in some money replacing it to get top dollar on eBay.

Item # 15: *Catcher's Gear*

Average Resale: $50- $100+

Difficult To Find: Medium

Final Note: When it comes to selling baseball catcher's gear I have found it most profitable to sell the complete set. When kids, teens, or even adults are shopping for catcher's gear, most of the times, they are looking for the complete set. Focus on brands such as Mizuno, All – Star, Nike, Louisville – Slugger, and Easton. Make sure there are no cracks in helmet, missing straps on leg guards, and missing material on the chest protector.

Chapter 6: Men's Boots

Item# 16: *Vasque*

Average Resale: $25- $75+

Difficult To Find: Medium

Final Note: These boots are in very high demand and are super high quality. You will usually find the sole of these boots made by Vibram. The gortex boots do the best, and can sell for some serious profits!

Item # 17: *Merrell*

Average Resale: $35- $75+

Difficult To Find: Easy - Medium

Final Note: Merrell is one of the most popular brands the market demands in terms of boots and has a terrific resale on eBay. There are many different models and styles, but in general, this brand does very well regardless of the type of footwear. If you find this brand pick it up!

Item # 18: *Doc Martens*

Average Resale: $25- $60+

Difficult To Find: Medium

Final Note: Doc Martens is one of my favorite brands to resell in terms of boots on eBay. This brand also does very well in terms of other types of footwear as well. Double check the edges of the boots to make sure the material is intact, I've had a few issues with this brand in terms of tearing of the material. Very profitable brand if in decent condition!

Chapter 7: Ties

Item# 19: *Brioni*

Average Resale: $20- $60+

Difficult To Find: Medium

Final Note: This is one of my favorite brands in terms of tie. Brioni is a high end Italian designer brand that makes a ton of high quality clothing and accessories. If you see the name Brioni you are in for some huge profits. The more interesting the design, and the more vibrant the colors, typically the better return you will receive on your investment!

Item # 20: *Robert Talbott*

Average Resale: $10- $30+

Difficult To Find: Easy -Medium

Final Note: When it comes to the Robert Talbott ties I like to stick to the ones that say "Best of Class". Also I find the ties within this brand that sell best have an interesting pattern or design that makes it stand out from the crowd!

Item # 21: *Vineyard Vines*

Average Resale: $20- $40

Difficult To Find: Medium- Hard

Final Note: Vineyard Vines is one of my all – time favorite brands to resell on eBay when it comes to clothing and clothing accessories. This brand may be hard to find at times, but if you find it, make sure you pick it up. These ties can retail for upward to $100.

Chapter 8: Books

Item# 22: *College Books*

Average Resale: $20-$100+

Difficult To Find: Medium

Final Note: When it comes to yielding some nice profits from college books you want to focus on the newer versions. Colleges are coming out with new issues and editions of textbooks every year, and if your book is too old, there is a good chance the value is very low. Look at the date in the inside of the book and look it up on the sold listings!

Item # 23: *Vintage Car Repair Manual Books*

Average Resale: $10-$50+

Difficult To Find: Hard

Final Note: The reason some of these old car manuals are worth so much money is because they are super hard to find. Owners of these vehicles who want to repair their cars need these and will be willing to pay whatever it costs to get their hands on the valuable information! If you find one of these you could be looking at some big money!

Item # 24: *Diet/ Health Books*

Average Resale: $5 - $50 +

Difficult To Find: Easy

Final Note: I advise when it comes to purchasing diet/health books to resell on eBay that you look them up first to see the selling history. Many of these books were mass produced which makes that practically worthless. I find that I have the best success selling these types of books around the New Year. Remember practically everyone is trying to lose weight for their new year's resolution. They need these types of book around that time!

Chapter 9: Hats

Item# 25: *Starter Snap Backs*

Average Resale: $20-$200+

Difficult To Find: Medium

Final Note: These starter hats can vary in price greatly due to the team, age of hat, and condition. Many customers who purchase these types of items on eBay are collectors, so be aware that condition can either make or break you in terms of your profits. One of my favorite teams to buy and sell is the Chicago bulls!

Item # 26: *Stetson Cowboy Hats*

Average Resale: $25 - $75+

Difficult To Find: Medium - Hard

Final Note: Stetson is one of the leading cowboy hat manufactures and is considered to be one of the best in the industry. The high quality hats are made with top of the line quality craftsmanship and the demand is high! Make sure the condition is good as I have noticed buyers are picky with these types of items!

Item # 27: Lacoste Hats

Average Resale: $20-$40

Difficult To Find: Medium

Final Note: These hats sell very quickly because they are in high demand. With that fact in mind you have to be very careful because many of these items are bootlegged and are counterfeit. Pay close attention to detail. If something seems off, odd, or not right, avoid the item because there is a good chance it is not authentic. Selling items that are faked on eBay is against policy and may cause you to be banned if caught. Buy with caution!

Bonus # 2: 10 Tips for making more money on eBay!

10 Bonus Tips for Making MORE Money on eBay

Tip # 1: *Source Thrift Stores on Sale Days*

If you want to maximize your profits while selling on eBay one of the best things you can do for your business is to acquire cheap inventory on sale days. If you are not sure whether or not your local thrift stores offer sale days, simple give them a call, and ask. Personally, where I live, my local thrift stores run half off days once a week, every Sunday. With the cost of shipping, eBay fees, supplies, PayPal and so on it is imperative you spend as little money possible when acquiring your inventory to resell.

Tip # 2: *Take Better Pictures*

Taking better pictures may be easier said than done, but to be honest, it's really not that hard to take excellent pictures. I won't go into too much detail here, but to be brief, all you need is a decent camera, a clean backdrop, proper lighting, and some basic editing software, and you are all set to take professional pictures. EBay even offers a free editing tool to clean up all your pictures.

Tip # 3: Add More Detail to Your eBay Listings

Adding the necessary details in your listing for a potential customer is huge! I have noticed that many sellers are very vague with their descriptions and don't go above and beyond in terms of item specifics. I think this is a huge mistake and takes a lot of sales away from the seller. Make sure to include the condition, size, measurements, any flaws, color, where item was produced, special selling points, or anything you feel the buyer may want to know to make a purchase right then and there.

Tip #4: Run Sales in Your Store

Running sales in your eBay store is huge because it will allow you to make more sales. Making more sales not only will make you more money , but it will shoot a signal to eBay's algorithm letting them know you are a good seller, and that buyers should see your items for sale. Also when running sales I have noticed my eBay listing rank higher in the search engine which is turn puts more eyes on my listings. As you know, the more traffic you get the more sales you will land!

Tip # 5: Improve Return Policy

Having a favorable return policy that makes your potential customers on eBay comfortable will work wonders for your business. Many sellers will put "No returns" in their listings and I find that this really throws up a red flag to buyers. If you are running a legitimate business on eBay and have faith in your products, then I feel you should take a leap of faith and accept returns. Of course, some people will take advantage of your return policy, using the item a few times, and then returning it, but in general, I have noticed most people are good people and won't take advantage of you. Plus if a buyer really wants a return all they have to do is start a claim with eBay and put forth " item not described" and they will get their money back anyways. Accept returns, trust me, it will help you make more money in the long run!

Tip # 6: Include a Thank You Letter

When I say a thank you letter I don't mean you have to actually write a letter, however, if you feel that motivated to do so then feel free! In all seriousness, all you have to do is include a little thank you card, sticker, or anything that let's your buyer know you appreciate their business. If you go onto eBay and type into the search bar "eBay thank you sticker" you will find the product I use to show my buyers appreciation. This will help you make your customers a lot happier, you will receive more positive feedback, and all in all, you will land more sales and make more money down the road!

Tip # 7: Offer the Best Customer Service You Can

Customer service is one of the major traits that will separate the winners from the losers in business. Look at some of the most success businesses in your local area. You will notice they go above and beyond for their customers to make them happy. Remember all it takes is one bad experience for one of your buyers to set off a chain reaction bad mouthing towards your business. Keep your customers happy and you will be much more successful in your eBay business!

Tip # 8: Ship Fast

In today's day of age people want to get the items they ordered super fast. Honestly, it's never fast enough! If you offer any more than 1 day shipping and handling time you are losing sales. You may think I am crazy to say that, but honestly, people are in a rush and want their stuff now! Offer 1 day shipping.

Tip # 9: Give Your Customers Free Shipping

Offering free shipping for your items for sale on eBay will not only intrigue buyer's to purchase from you, but it will also rank your listings higher in the search engine. On top of that, it will help you to become a top rated seller. There are tons of benefits to offering free shipping. You need to be doing this!

Tip # 10: Create A Listing Schedule and Follow Through

Now that you have your business in line and you are ready to be making a lot of money on a consistent basis, now you have to create a listing schedule. The only way you will make money from the items you find at thrift stores, garage sales, and flea markets is to actually list them on eBay. You won't believe how many people miss this step! It's crazy! In order to create a listing schedule take a look at the opening in time you have free to list and make a commitment. I list everyday for at least 2-3 hours. Listings consistently will help you to make a lot more money!http://www.projectlifemastery.com/

CPSIA information can be obtained
at www.ICGtesting.com
Printed in the USA
LVOW13s1811020117
519456LV00019B/1300/P